PICTORIAL ARCHIVE OF GEOMETRIC DESIGNS

WIL STEGENGA

DOVER PUBLICATIONS, INC., New York

Published in Canada by General Publishing Company, Ltd., 30 Lesmill Road, Don Mills, Toronto, Ontario.
Published in the United Kingdom by Constable and Company, Ltd., 3 The Lanchesters, 162–164 Fulham Palace Road, London W6 9ER.

Pictorial Archive of Geometric Designs is a new work, first published by Dover Publications, Inc., in 1992.

DOVER *Pictorial Archive* SERIES

Manufactured in the United States of America
Dover Publications, Inc., 31 East 2nd Street, Mineola, N.Y. 11501

Library of Congress Cataloging-in-Publication Data

Stegenga, Wil.
    Pictorial archive of geometric designs / Wil Stegenga.
        p.   cm. — (Dover pictorial archive series)
    ISBN 0-486-27148-X
    1. Stegenga, Wil. 2. Repetitive patterns (Decorative arts) I. Title.
II. Series.
NK1535.S74A4   1992
745.4′492—dc20   92-13990
                                                          CIP

NOTE

This volume contains 260 of artist Wil Stegenga's original geometric designs. These compositions are remarkable for the breadth and inventiveness they display within the constraints of formalized contour and the absence of color. Individual designs explore a variety of perceptual and graphic possibilities, ranging from patterns of calming symmetry and pleasing balance to challenging networks of form and contrast that push vision to its limits.

In its entirety, this collection forms a visual treatise on the calculated manipulation of shape and pattern, containing many one-of-a-kind designs as well as groups that treat similar elements differently. As such, it is of interest both as a visual tool and resource for artists and designers and as a unique portfolio of original works.

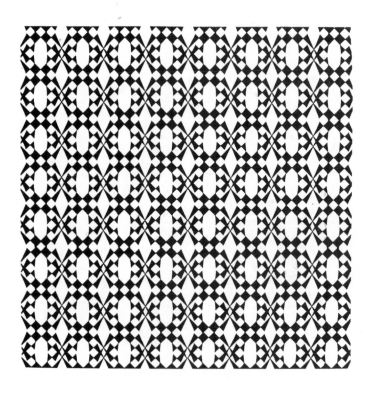
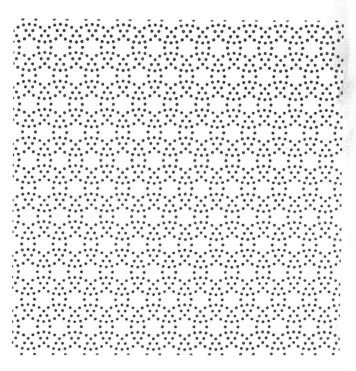
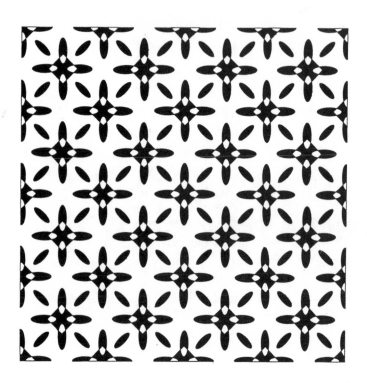
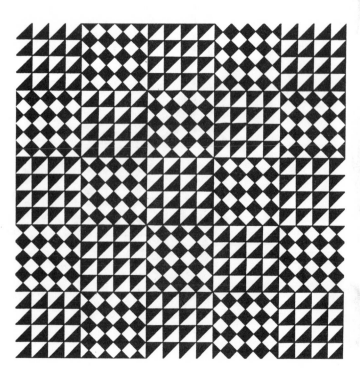

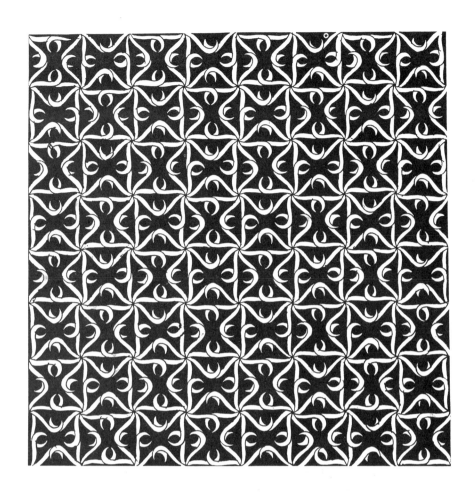

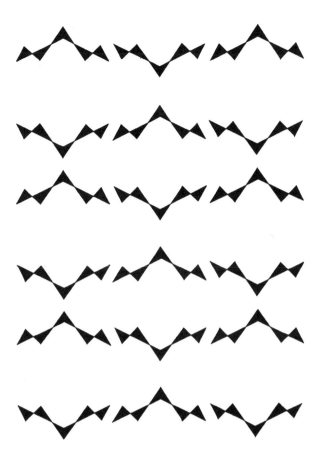

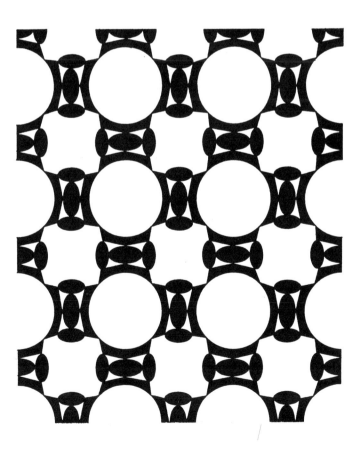

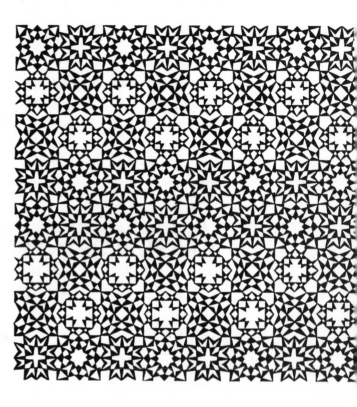
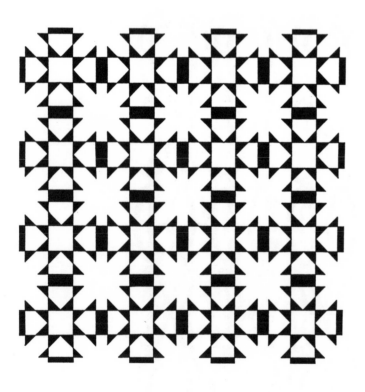
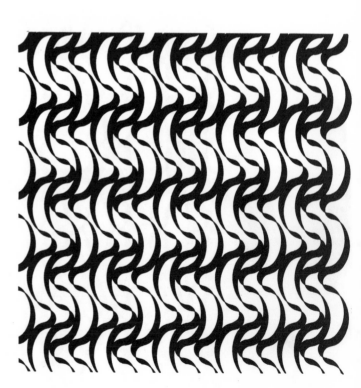

13

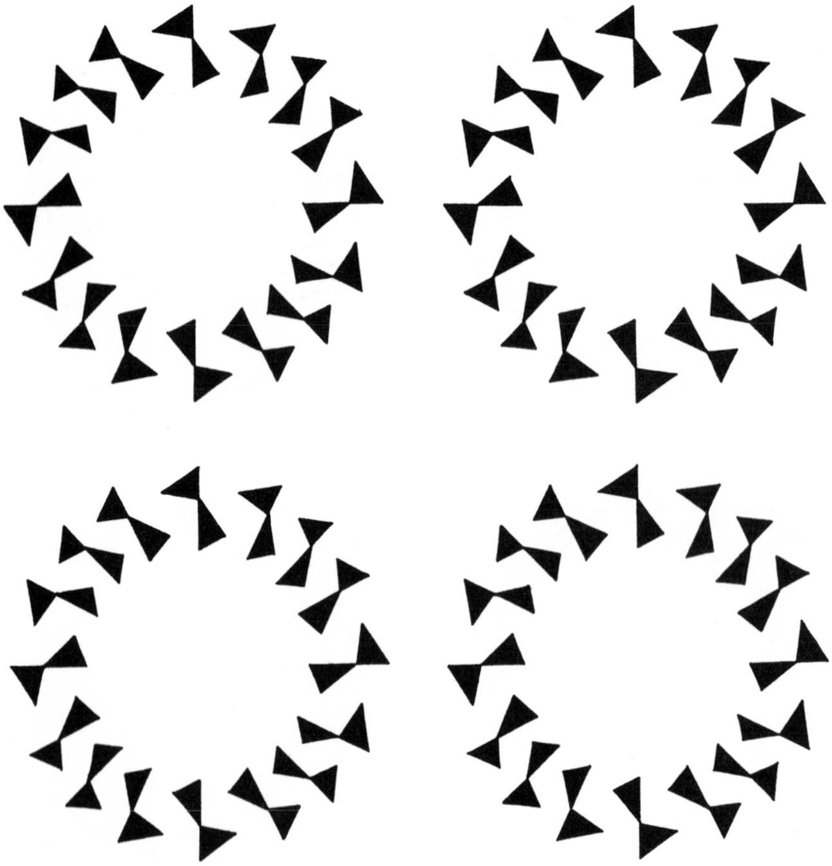

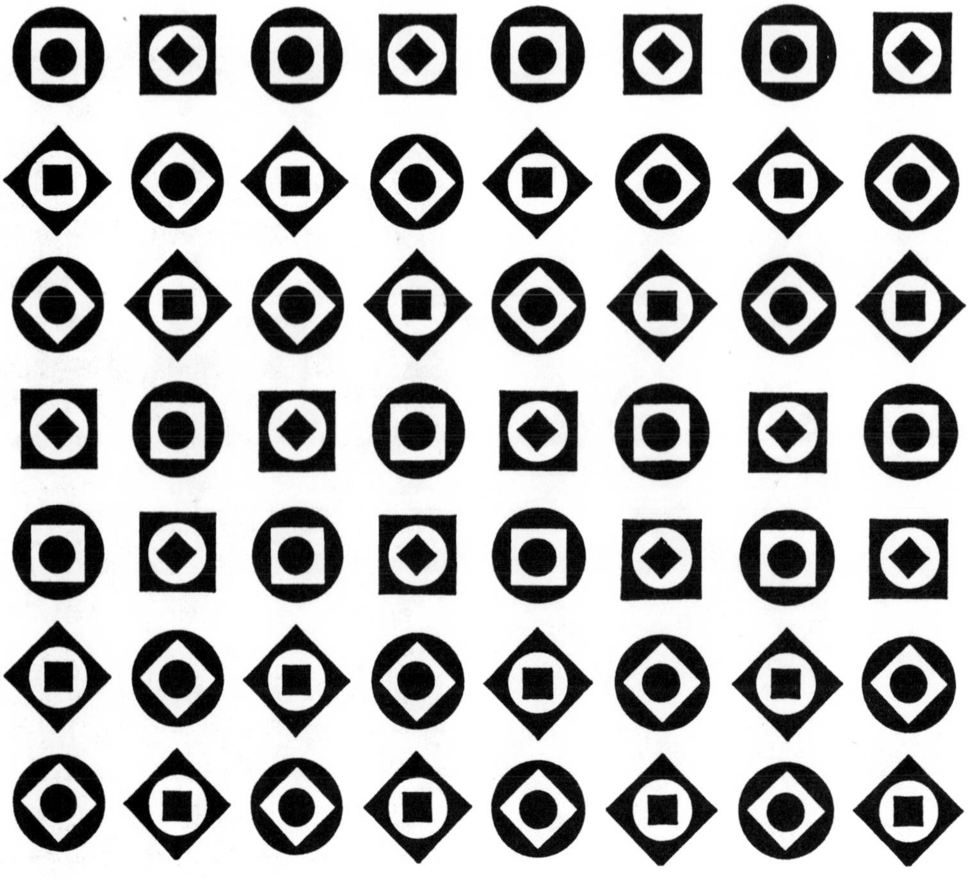

15

19

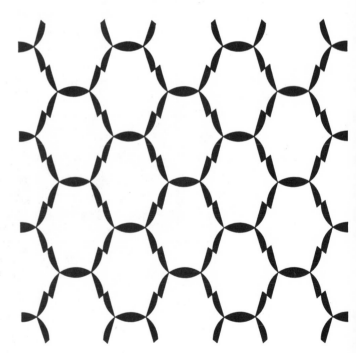

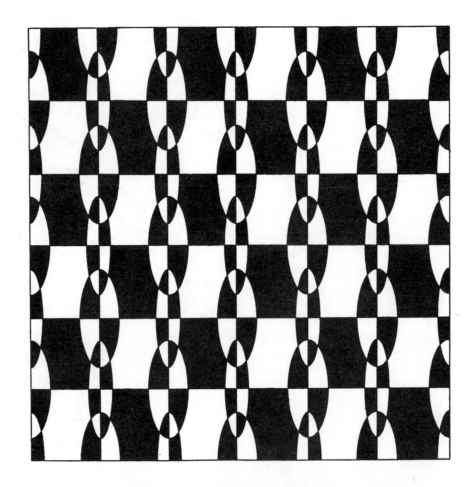

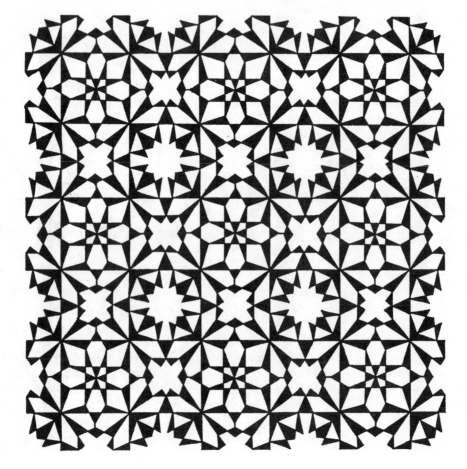

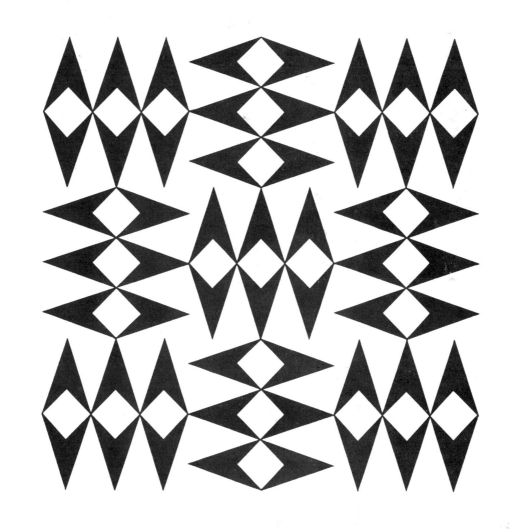

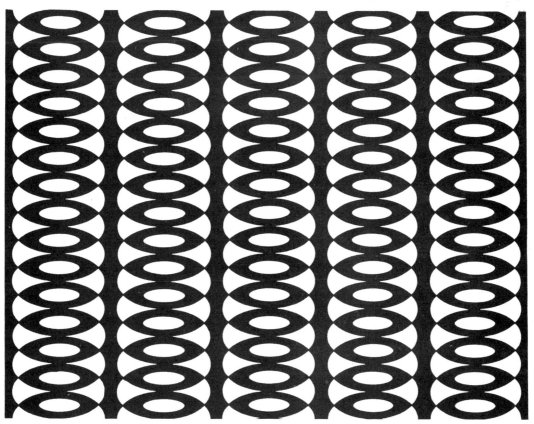

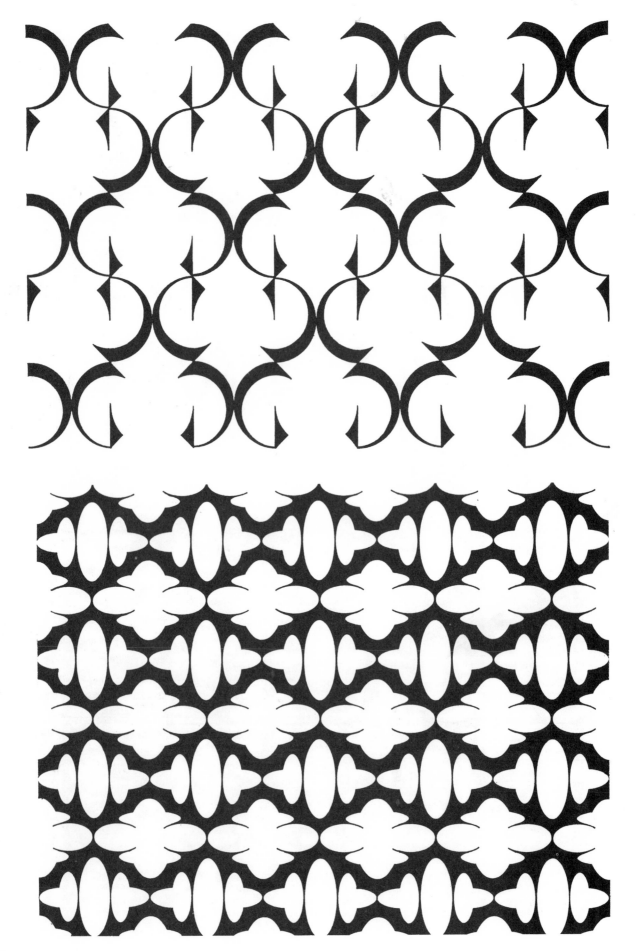

26

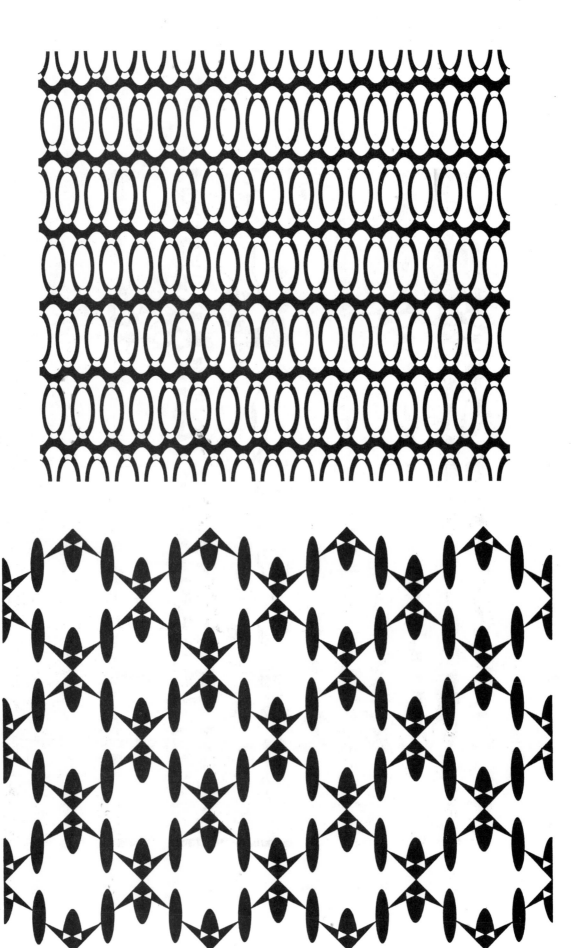

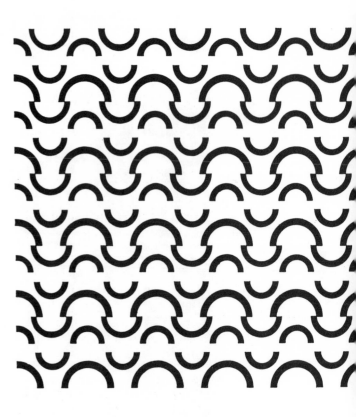

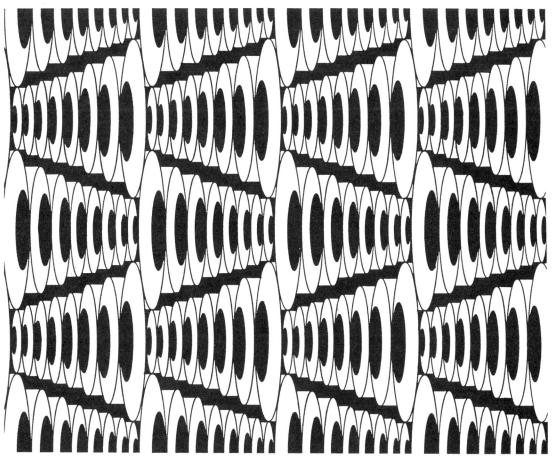

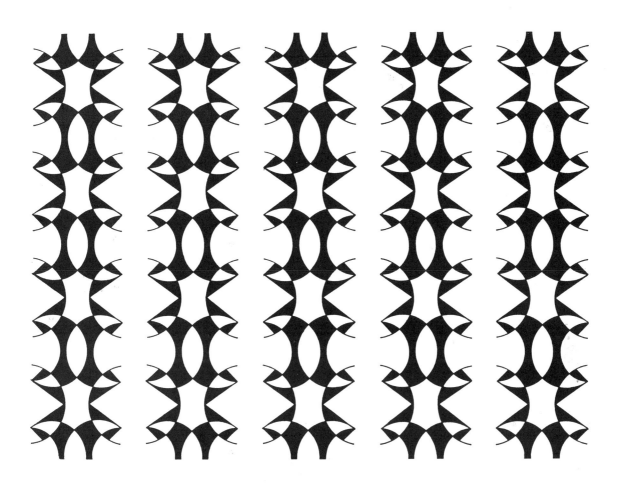

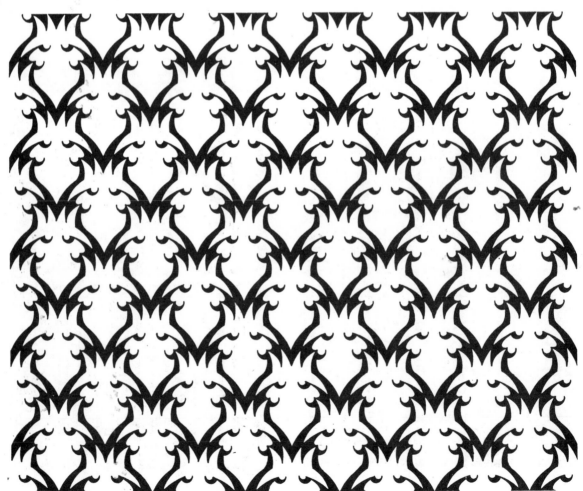

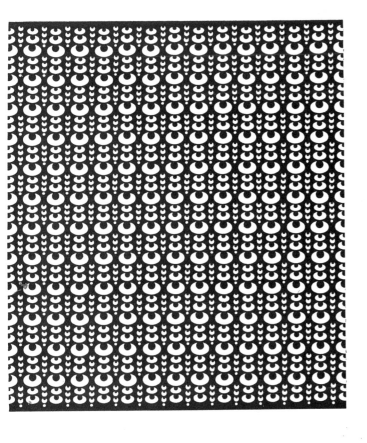

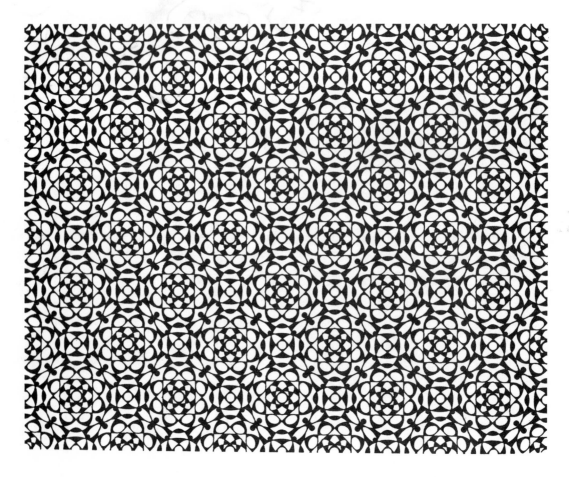

38

41

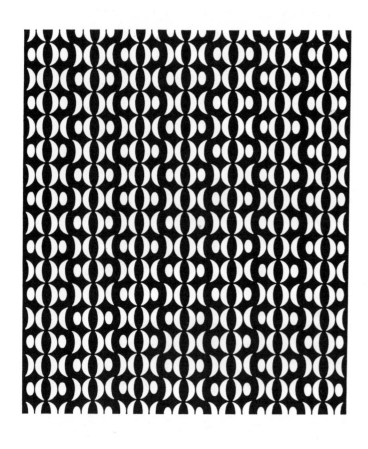

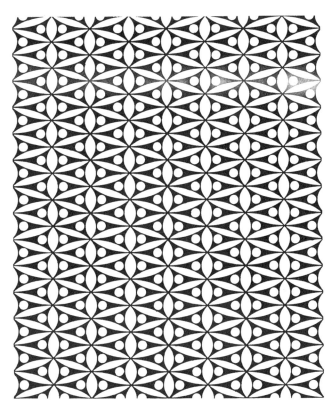

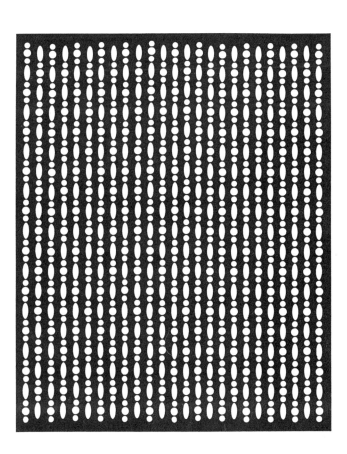

46

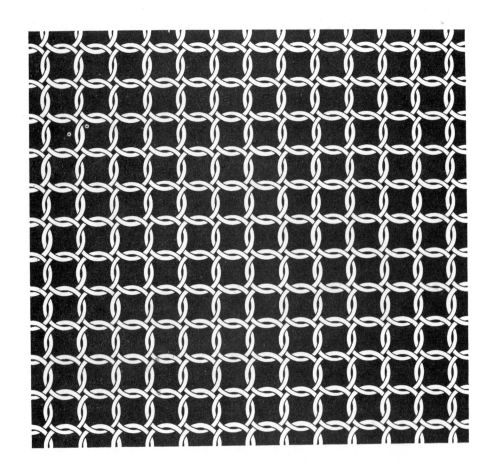

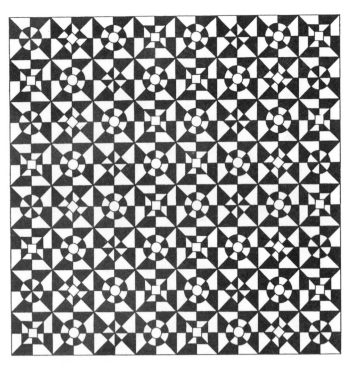

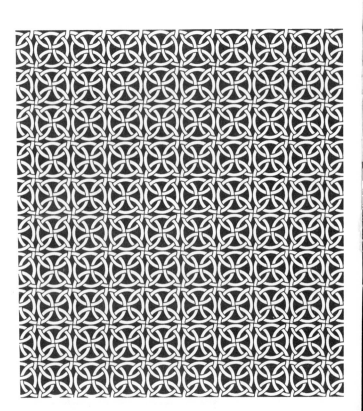

63

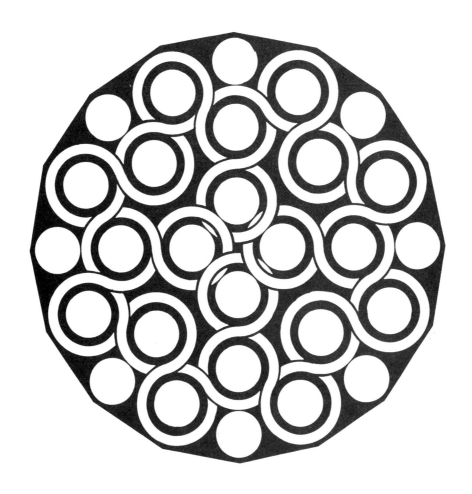

74

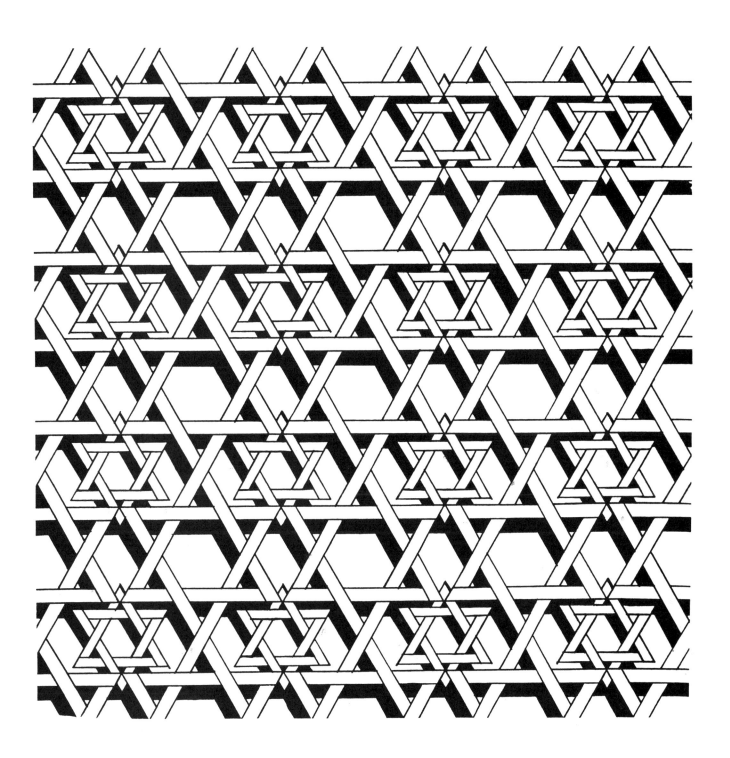

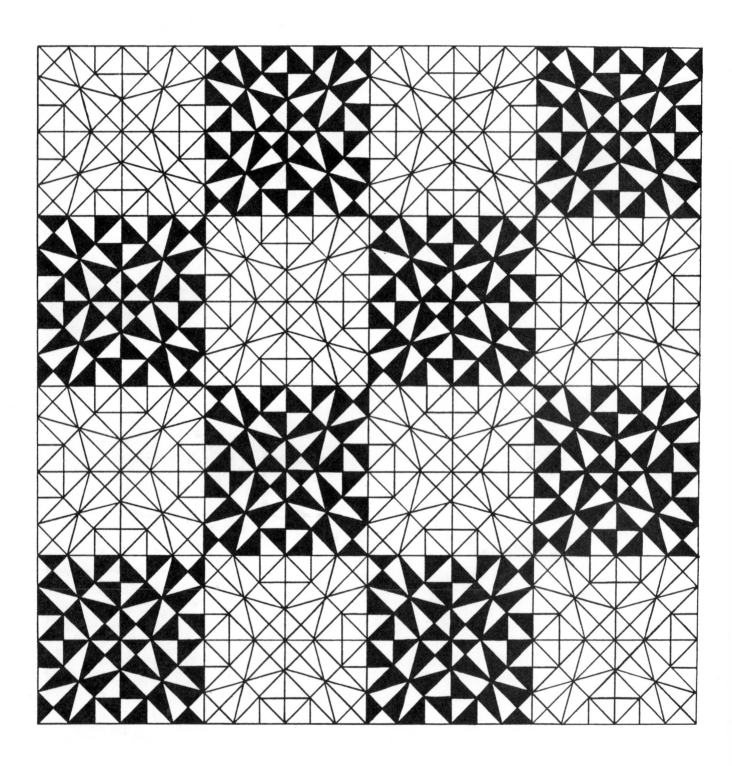

78

83

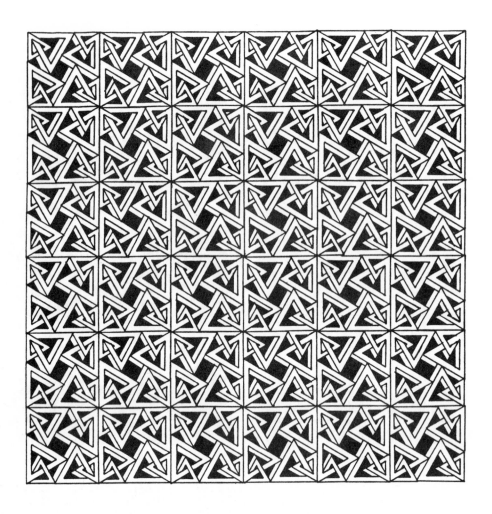

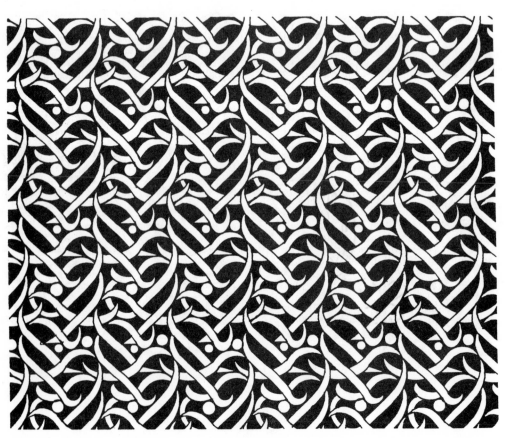

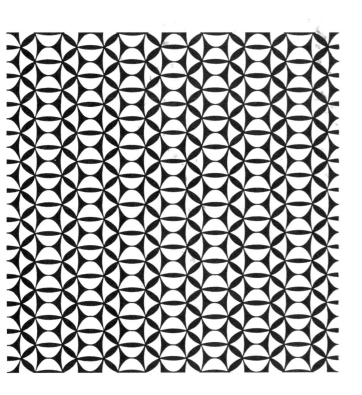

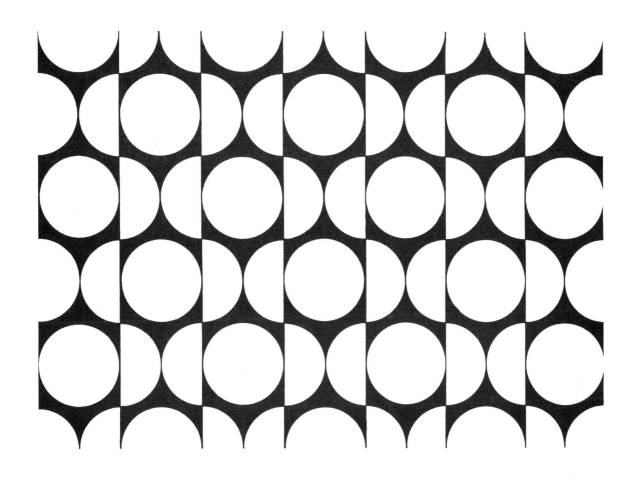

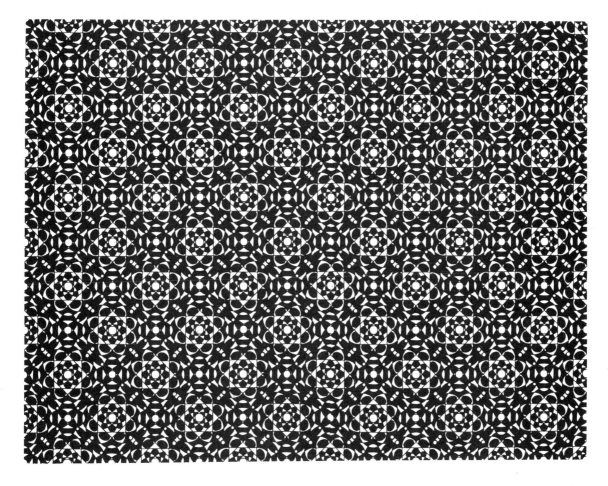

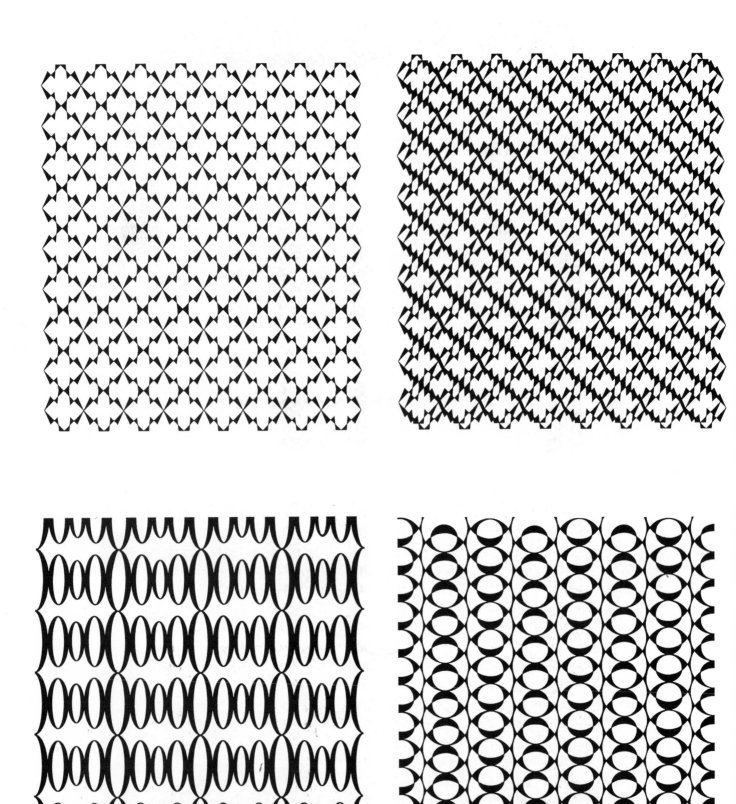

94

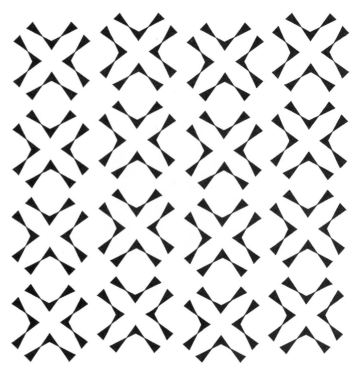

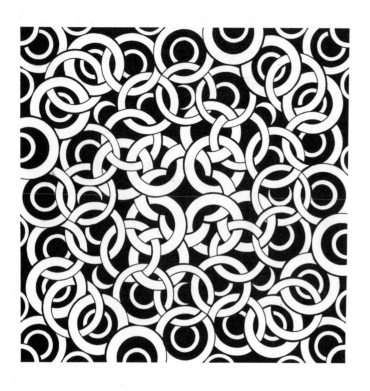

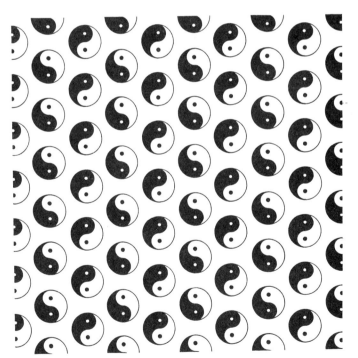

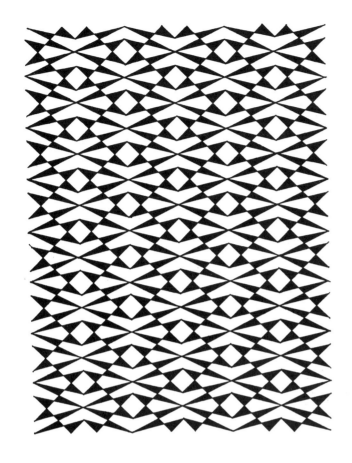

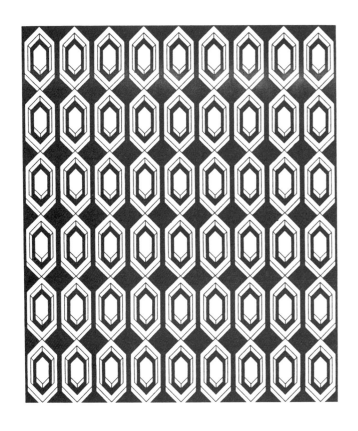

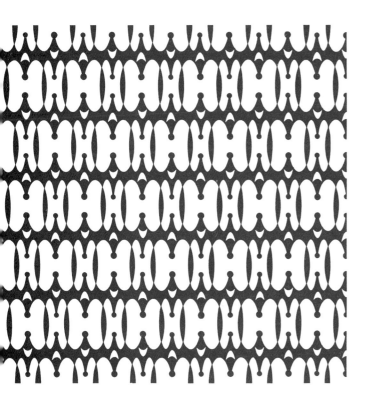

111

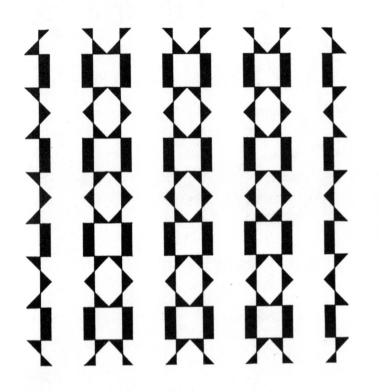

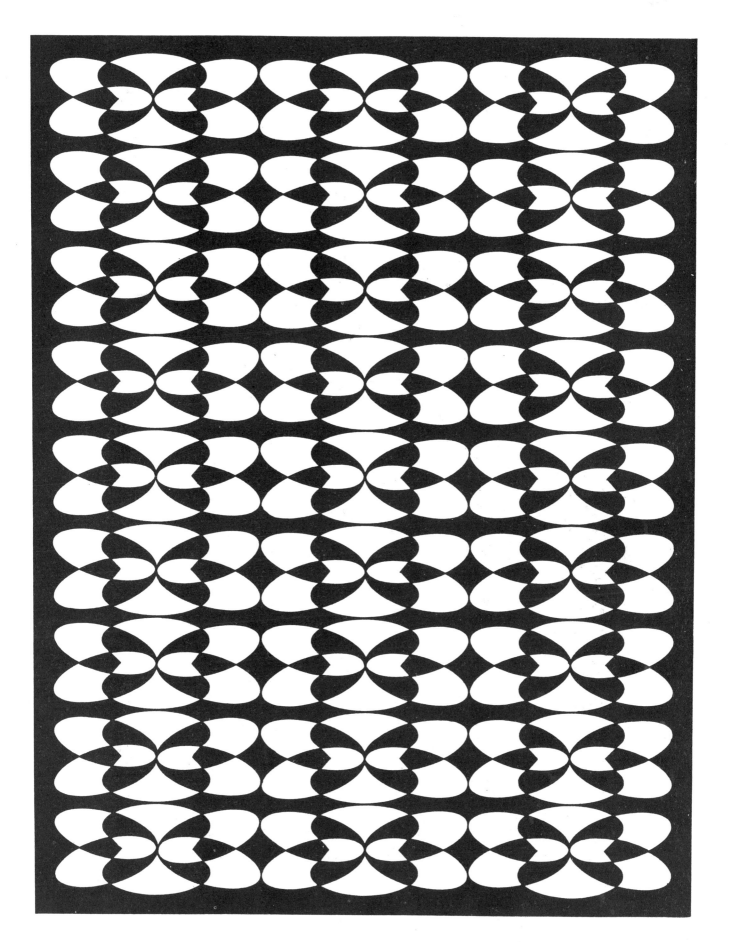

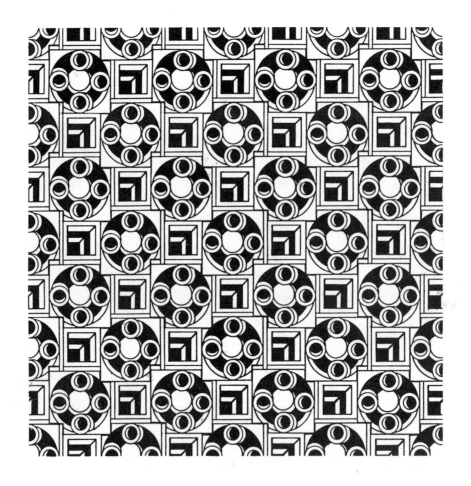

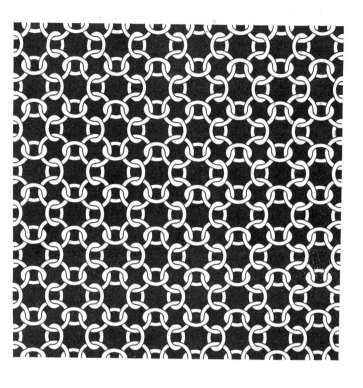

116

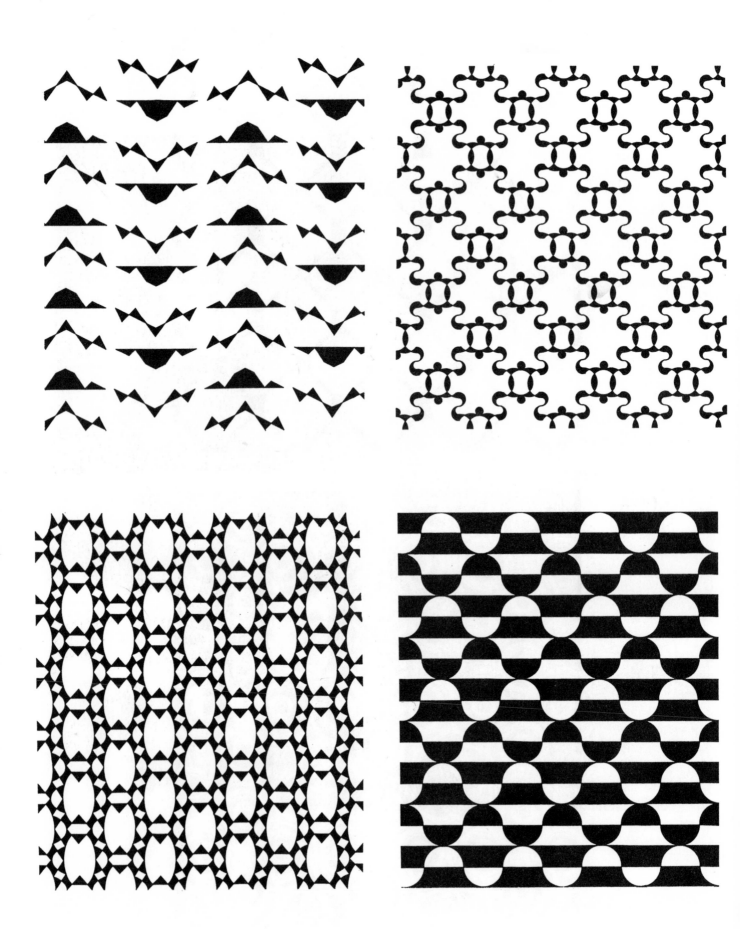

119

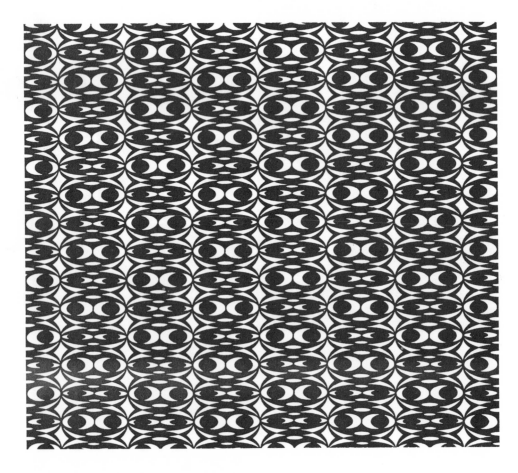